Table of Contents

Introduction..1
Chapter 1: Introduction to Virtual Assistance..........5
Chapter 2: Assessing Your Skills and Services.... 10
Chapter 3: Setting Up Your Virtual Assistant Business...14
Chapter 4: Finding Your First Clients....................20
Chapter 5: Establishing Your Pricing and Packages. 24
Chapter 6: Onboarding Clients and Managing Projects..28
Chapter 7: Delivering High-Quality Services.........33
Chapter 8: Scaling Your Virtual Assistant Business.. 37
Chapter 9: Navigating Challenges and Overcoming Obstacles...43
Chapter 10: Sustaining Success and Long-Term Growth..48
Conclusion: Embracing the Future as a Virtual Assistant..52

Introduction

Welcome to "The Ultimate Guide on How to Start a Virtual Assistant Business"! This book is your comprehensive resource for navigating the dynamic world of virtual assistance. Whether you're new to the industry or looking to expand your existing business, we've got you covered with all the knowledge and tools you'll need to build a successful venture in this thriving field.

Why Choose Virtual Assistance?

With technology advancing rapidly and the demand for flexible work arrangements on the rise, virtual assistance has become a highly sought-after service. Here are some compelling reasons to consider starting a virtual assistant business:

1. **Freedom and Flexibility:** One of the biggest perks of being a virtual assistant is the ability to set your own working hours and choose your work location. Imagine working from the comfort of your home, or even while traveling the world, as long as you have a stable internet connection.
2. **Low Startup Costs:** Unlike traditional businesses, starting a virtual assistant business doesn't require a hefty investment. You won't need to rent office

space or buy expensive equipment. All you need is a computer, an internet connection, and some essential software tools to get started.
3. **Variety of Services:** As a virtual assistant, you can offer a wide range of services, from administrative tasks to digital marketing, social media management, bookkeeping, and more. This versatility allows you to leverage your existing skills or even learn new ones to serve a diverse client base.
4. **High Demand:** With more businesses relying on remote workforces, the demand for virtual assistants is steadily increasing. Entrepreneurs, small business owners, and professionals from various industries are constantly seeking virtual assistants to streamline their operations and reduce their workload.

What You'll Learn

This book will guide you through each step of starting and growing your virtual assistant business, ensuring you have the knowledge and confidence to succeed. Here's a sneak peek at what you'll learn in each chapter:

- **Chapter 1: Introduction to Virtual Assistance**

Gain a comprehensive understanding of the virtual assistant industry, its benefits, and the essential skills needed to thrive in this profession.

- **Chapter 2: Assessing Your Skills and Services**
Evaluate your existing skills, identify your niche, and determine the services you will offer as a virtual assistant.
- **Chapter 3: Setting Up Your Virtual Assistant Business**
Learn how to legally establish your business, create a professional brand, set up a home office, and acquire the necessary tools and resources.
- **Chapter 4: Finding Your First Clients**
Discover effective strategies to find your initial clients, build relationships, and establish a strong client base.
- **Chapter 5: Establishing Your Pricing and Packages**
Understand different pricing models, how to package your services, and set competitive prices that reflect the value you provide.
- **Chapter 6: Onboarding Clients and Managing Projects**
Learn how to effectively onboard clients, establish clear communication channels, and manage projects efficiently to exceed client expectations.

- **Chapter 7: Delivering High-Quality Services**
  Master the art of delivering exceptional services to your clients, ensuring their satisfaction and fostering long-term relationships.
- **Chapter 8: Scaling Your Virtual Assistant Business**
  Explore strategies to scale your business, hire and manage a team, and expand your service offerings to cater to a larger client base.
- **Chapter 9: Navigating Challenges and Overcoming Obstacles**
  Identify common challenges faced by virtual assistants and learn how to overcome them to maintain a thriving business.
- **Chapter 10: Sustaining Success and Long-Term Growth**
  Discover strategies to sustain success, continuously improve your skills, and achieve long-term growth in your virtual assistant business.

Whether you're just starting in the virtual assistance industry or looking to enhance your existing business, this book is your ultimate guide to building a profitable and fulfilling virtual assistant business. So, let's dive in and embark on this exciting journey together!

Chapter 1: Introduction to Virtual Assistance

Welcome to the world of virtual assistance, a booming industry that's been growing rapidly in recent years. Thanks to the advancements in technology and the increasing trend towards remote work, entrepreneurs everywhere are discovering the many perks of hiring virtual assistants to help them manage their businesses more efficiently.

Understanding Virtual Assistance

So, what exactly is virtual assistance? In a nutshell, it's a profession where people provide a variety of administrative, technical, or creative services to clients from a remote location. This setup allows business owners to delegate tasks they don't have time for, freeing them up to focus on more strategic aspects of their operations. Virtual assistants (VAs) can handle a wide range of duties, including but not limited to:

Administrative Support

Imagine having someone to manage your emails, schedule your appointments, make travel arrangements, and organize your files—all without needing to be in the same room as you. That's what a VA can do for you.

Customer Service

Need someone to provide support to your customers, answer their inquiries, and handle any complaints or issues? A virtual assistant can do that too, ensuring your customers are happy and well taken care of.

Social Media Management

Keeping up with social media can be time-consuming. A VA can create and schedule posts, manage your accounts, and engage with your followers, helping to build your brand's online presence.

Content Creation

Got creative skills? VAs can help write blog posts, create graphics, edit videos, and develop marketing materials. Basically, they can help you get your message out there in a way that looks professional and polished.

The Advantages of Virtual Assistance

Now, let's talk about why virtual assistance is such a great option for entrepreneurs. Here are some key benefits:

Cost-Effective

Hiring a VA means you don't have to worry about providing office space, equipment, or employee benefits. Most virtual assistants are self-employed and cover their own expenses, saving you money.

Flexibility
You can hire a VA on an as-needed basis or for specific projects. This flexibility allows you to scale up or down depending on your business needs, without the long-term commitment of a full-time employee.

Access to Diverse Skills
VAs come from all sorts of backgrounds and possess a wide range of skills. This means you can find someone with the exact expertise you need for your business, whether it's technical know-how, creative talent, or administrative prowess.

Increased Productivity
By delegating administrative and non-core tasks to a VA, you can focus your time and energy on the most important aspects of your business. This not only boosts your productivity but also helps your business grow faster.

Is Virtual Assistance Right for You?

Before jumping into the virtual assistant industry, it's important to assess whether it's the right fit for you. Here are a few things to consider:

Skills and Experience
Take a look at your skills and experience. Do they align with the services typically offered by VAs? If you have experience in administrative tasks, customer service, or other relevant areas, virtual assistance could be a great career path for you.

Self-Motivation and Discipline
Working as a VA requires a high level of self-motivation and discipline. You'll need to manage your time effectively, meet deadlines, and prioritize tasks without direct supervision. If you're someone who can stay focused and organized on your own, this could be a great fit.

Desire for Flexibility
Do you value flexibility in your work schedule? Do you enjoy working from the comfort of your own home? If so, virtual assistance offers a fantastic opportunity for a better work-life balance and the chance to work with clients from around the world.

Entrepreneurial Spirit
Many VAs work with multiple clients or manage their own businesses. Having an entrepreneurial spirit and a desire to grow and develop your skills can greatly contribute to your success in this industry.

Conclusion

Virtual assistance offers a world of opportunities for both entrepreneurs looking for help and individuals seeking a rewarding and flexible career. In the upcoming chapters, we'll dive deeper into the various aspects of starting and running a successful virtual assistant business. So, buckle up and get ready to explore this exciting field!

Chapter 2: Assessing Your Skills and Services

Starting a virtual assistant business is an exciting journey, but before you dive in, it's important to have a clear understanding of your skills and the services you can offer. In this chapter, we'll walk through the steps to evaluate your abilities and define your service offerings. This will help ensure that you are well-prepared to meet the needs of potential clients and stand out in the competitive market of virtual assistance.

Evaluate Your Skill Set

First things first, let's talk about your skills. Before you can effectively market yourself as a virtual assistant, you need to have a good grasp of what you're bringing to the table. Here are some key questions to consider:

1. **What are your core competencies?**
   Think about the skills you excel in and have significant experience with. These are your strengths and will form the foundation of your service offerings.
2. **What tasks do you enjoy doing the most?**
   Reflect on the tasks that bring you the most satisfaction. It's important to choose services that you enjoy because

you'll be more motivated and effective in your work.
3. **What skills do you need to improve or acquire?**
Identify any gaps in your skill set. Are there areas where you could use more training or experience? Investing time to enhance these skills will broaden the range of services you can offer.

Remember, virtual assistants can offer a wide array of services such as administrative support, customer service, social media management, and content creation. By thoroughly evaluating your skills, you can focus on the services you can deliver most effectively.

Define Your Service Offerings

Now that you have a clear understanding of your skills, it's time to define your service offerings. This involves a few strategic steps:

1. **Research the market:**
Look into the demand for different virtual assistant services within your target market. Identify which services are in high demand and see how they align with your skills and interests.
2. **Determine your niche:**
Specializing in a specific area or

industry can help you stand out. By becoming an expert in a niche, you can attract clients who are looking for specialized services and are willing to pay a premium for expertise.
3. **Decide on your service packages:** Think about the specific services you will offer and how you can package them. For instance, you might offer a basic administrative support package and a more comprehensive package that includes social media management or content creation. Creating different pricing tiers can help you cater to a variety of client needs.
4. **Set your pricing:** Determine your pricing structure by considering the complexity of tasks, the value you provide, and industry standards. Research what other virtual assistants are charging to ensure your prices are competitive.
5. **Create a compelling service list:** Develop a clear and attractive list of services you offer. Highlight the benefits and value clients can expect when they work with you. Make sure to communicate your unique selling points and how your services can meet their specific needs.

Conclusion

Assessing your skills and defining your service offerings are critical steps in building a successful virtual assistant business. Take the time to evaluate your strengths, identify areas for improvement, and align your services with market demand. By doing so, you'll be well-positioned to attract clients who appreciate the expertise and value you bring to their businesses. This thoughtful preparation will set you on the path to success in your virtual assistant journey.

Chapter 3: Setting Up Your Virtual Assistant Business

Starting a virtual assistant business is an exciting venture, but it does require careful planning and preparation. In this chapter, we'll walk you through the essential steps to get your virtual assistant business up and running, from choosing the right business structure to creating a professional brand. So, let's dive in and get started!

Choosing a Business Structure

The first step in setting up your virtual assistant business is deciding on the right business structure. This decision is crucial because it affects your legal and financial responsibilities. There are several options to consider:

- **Sole Proprietorship:** This is the simplest and most common structure for small businesses. As a sole proprietor, you are the sole owner and responsible for all aspects of the business. However, this also means you are personally liable for any debts or legal issues.
- **Partnership:** If you're starting your business with someone else, a partnership might be the way to go. This structure allows you to share

responsibilities and profits, but it also means sharing liabilities.
- **Limited Liability Company (LLC):** An LLC offers a good balance between flexibility and protection. It provides limited liability protection, meaning your personal assets are generally protected from business debts and claims.
- **Corporation:** Forming a corporation can provide the highest level of personal liability protection, but it also comes with more regulations and higher administrative costs.

Each structure has its own set of advantages and disadvantages, so it's important to research and understand them thoroughly. You might also want to consult with a legal or financial professional to determine which option is best for your situation.

Registering Your Business

Once you've chosen a business structure, the next step is to register your business. The registration process can vary depending on your location, so it's essential to check with your local government agencies for specific requirements. Here's a general outline of what you might need to do:

1. **Register Your Business Name:** Choose a unique name for your business that reflects your services and appeals to your target audience. Make sure to conduct a thorough search to ensure the name isn't already in use.
2. **Obtain Necessary Permits and Licenses:** Depending on your location and the services you offer, you might need specific permits or licenses to operate legally.
3. **Register for Taxes:** You'll need to apply for an Employer Identification Number (EIN) from the IRS if you're in the United States, which is used for tax purposes.

Creating a Professional Brand

To stand out in the competitive virtual assistant industry, creating a professional brand is essential. Here's how you can do it:

1. **Choose a Business Name:** Your business name should reflect your services and resonate with your target audience. Once you've settled on a name, register it as a domain name for your website.
2. **Design a Logo:** A logo is a visual representation of your brand. Invest in a professional design that's simple,

memorable, and reflects the essence of your business.
3. **Create a Website:** Your website is your online storefront. It should showcase your services, experience, and testimonials from satisfied clients. Make sure it includes a clear and concise description of your services and easy-to-find contact information.
4. **Consider Trademarking:** If you want to protect your brand name and logo, consider trademarking them. This can prevent others from using your brand identity.

Setting Up Your Office

As a virtual assistant, your office will be the central hub of your business. Here are some tips for setting up an efficient workspace:

1. **Choose a Quiet, Comfortable Area:** Find a space where you can focus and minimize distractions. This could be a dedicated room in your home or a quiet corner.
2. **Invest in Essential Equipment:** Make sure you have a reliable computer, high-speed internet connection, printer, and phone system. These tools are crucial for providing

seamless virtual assistance to your clients.
3. **Organize Your Space:** Keep your workspace tidy and organized. This can help boost your productivity and make your work environment more pleasant

Establishing Business Policies and Procedures

Setting clear business policies and procedures is crucial for running a successful virtual assistant business. Here's what you need to do:

1. **Create a Client Agreement:** Draft a comprehensive client agreement that outlines the scope of work, payment terms, confidentiality provisions, and other important details. This will protect both you and your clients and ensure a smooth working relationship.
2. **Develop Standard Operating Procedures (SOPs):** Create SOPs for common tasks and processes. This will help streamline your workflow and ensure consistency in delivering high-quality services. SOPs will also be invaluable if you decide to hire subcontractors or grow your team in the future.

Conclusion

Setting up your virtual assistant business involves making important decisions about your business structure, registering your business, creating a professional brand, setting up your office, and establishing business policies and procedures. By taking the time to carefully plan and prepare, you'll lay a solid foundation for your virtual assistant business and increase your chances of long-term success. So, take it step by step, and you'll be well on your way to building a thriving virtual assistant business!

Chapter 4: Finding Your First Clients

Starting a virtual assistant business is an exciting venture, but one of the first and most crucial steps is finding your first clients. It's all about developing effective strategies to attract and secure clients who will trust and value your services. In this chapter, we'll dive into different methods and approaches to help you acquire those first clients and build a strong client base.

1. Leverage Your Network

Begin by reaching out to people you already know. Let your friends, family, and colleagues know about your new virtual assistant services and ask if they can refer anyone who might need your help. Word-of-mouth recommendations are incredibly powerful because people trust referrals from those they know personally.

Don't stop there, though. Attend networking events, both online and in person. These gatherings are golden opportunities to connect with potential clients and to showcase your skills and expertise. Even a casual mention at a social event could lead to a valuable connection.

2. Utilize Online Platforms

The internet is a treasure trove of opportunities for finding clients. There are numerous websites designed to connect clients with virtual assistants, such as Upwork, Freelancer, and Fiverr. Make sure to create a professional profile on these platforms. Highlight your skills, experience, and the services you offer. Including examples of your work and testimonials from satisfied clients can significantly boost your credibility.

Additionally, consider using professional networking sites like LinkedIn. Build a strong profile that highlights your expertise, and actively engage in relevant groups and discussions. This will increase your visibility and help attract potential clients who are looking for virtual assistant services.

3. Establish an Online Presence

Creating an online presence is essential for attracting clients. Start with a professional website that showcases your services, your expertise, and client testimonials. Optimize your website for search engines (SEO) to ensure it shows up when potential clients search for virtual assistants.

Sharing valuable content related to virtual assistance through a blog or social media can also help. This not only demonstrates your expertise but also attracts potential clients. Utilize social media platforms like Facebook,

Twitter, and Instagram to connect with potential clients. Join relevant groups and communities, and actively engage with posts and discussions. This will help you establish yourself as a knowledgeable and trustworthy virtual assistant.

4. Attend Industry-Specific Conferences and Events

Industry-specific conferences and events are fantastic places to network with potential clients and industry professionals. These events give you a platform to showcase your expertise, learn from industry leaders, and gain insights into the needs and challenges of your target market.

To make the most of these opportunities, consider volunteering as a speaker, hosting workshops, or setting up a booth. These activities will allow you to interact directly with potential clients and establish yourself as a trusted authority in the field of virtual assistance.

5. Offer Special Promotions and Incentives

Everyone loves a good deal. To attract your first clients, think about offering special promotions or incentives. This could be discounted rates for the first few clients, referral bonuses, or package deals. Such offers can encourage potential clients to choose your services over those of your competitors, helping you to build a strong initial client base.

Conclusion

Finding your first clients is a significant milestone in establishing your virtual assistant business. By leveraging your network, utilizing online platforms, establishing an online presence, attending industry-specific events, and offering special promotions, you can attract potential clients. With persistence and determination, you'll draw in clients who value your expertise and build a solid foundation for long-term success.

Chapter 5: Establishing Your Pricing and Packages

Setting the right pricing and packaging structure for your virtual assistant services is a crucial step in establishing your business. It not only determines your earning potential but also communicates the value you provide to your clients. In this chapter, we will explore various factors to consider when establishing your pricing and packages to ensure your business thrives.

Determine Your Value

Before setting your prices, it's essential to assess the value you offer to your clients. Consider factors such as your experience, expertise, and the outcomes or results you can deliver. Understanding your value proposition will help you differentiate yourself from competitors and justify your rates to potential clients.

Evaluate Market Rates

Researching market rates is vital in ensuring your pricing remains competitive. Begin by investigating the rates charged by other virtual assistants who offer similar services to yours. Look for professionals with similar credentials and experience levels to get an accurate understanding of what clients are willing to pay. However, keep in mind that pricing too low could undermine the value you provide and potentially attract clients who don't appreciate your expertise. On the other hand, pricing too high might deter potential clients. It's crucial to strike a balance where your rates align with market expectations while reflecting your skills and experience.

Create Service Packages

Service packages streamline your offerings and make it easier for clients to understand and choose the services they require. When creating your packages, consider the various tasks you specialize in and how they can be bundled together to provide value. Divide your services into different packages based on complexity, time commitment, and deliverables. Start with a basic package that includes essential services and offer additional add-ons or customization options for clients who require more comprehensive assistance. Think about the needs of different client types, such as entrepreneurs, small businesses, or professionals in specific industries. Tailor your packages to suit their requirements, ensuring that they address their pain points effectively.

Set Your Pricing Structure

When determining your pricing structure, consider factors like your operational costs, the time it takes to complete tasks, and the perceived value of your services. You can establish your pricing based on an hourly rate, project rate, or a retainer fee.

- **Hourly Rate:** This pricing model involves charging clients for the hours you work on their tasks. Set an hourly rate that reflects your value and covers your expenses while remaining competitive in the market.
- **Project Rate:** If you prefer a more standardized approach, consider charging clients a fixed rate for specific projects. This pricing model allows you to estimate the time and resources required accurately.
- **Retainer Fee:** Another option is to offer retainer packages where clients pay a set fee per month for a specified number of hours or a package of services. This model offers predictability for both you and your clients.

Avoid Scope Creep

Scope creep refers to the gradual expansion of tasks beyond the original agreement without appropriate compensation. To prevent scope creep, clearly define the boundaries and limitations for each package. Communicate any additional charges for tasks outside the scope of the original agreement. Regularly review the services you offer and update your packages and pricing accordingly, considering changes in demand and market trends. This flexibility ensures that you stay competitive and meet the evolving needs of your clients.

Conclusion: Establishing Your Pricing and Packages

Establishing your pricing and packages is not a one-time task but an ongoing process. It requires careful consideration of your value, market rates, and the needs of your target clients. By creating well-defined packages and pricing structures, you can attract clients who appreciate your expertise and build a sustainable and profitable virtual assistant business.

Chapter 6: Onboarding Clients and Managing Projects

Welcome to Chapter 6! Now that you've successfully attracted clients to your virtual assistant business, the next crucial step is to onboard them effectively and manage their projects efficiently. This chapter will guide you through the process of onboarding clients and offer valuable insights on managing projects to ensure client satisfaction and build long-term partnerships.

The Importance of Onboarding

Onboarding clients is more than just a simple welcome; it's a golden opportunity to set the tone for the entire working relationship. A well-executed onboarding process establishes clear communication channels, aligns expectations, and ensures a smooth transition into working together. Effective onboarding also instills confidence in your clients, reaffirming their decision to choose your services.

Developing an Onboarding Process

To streamline the onboarding process, consider developing a standardized procedure that can be customized for each client. This process should include the following steps:

1. **Welcome Package:** Prepare a comprehensive welcome package that introduces your business, provides an overview of your services, and includes relevant documents such as a client agreement or contract.
2. **Kick-off Meeting:** Schedule a kick-off meeting with your client to discuss project details, expectations, timelines, and any specific requirements. This meeting is an excellent opportunity to build rapport and clarify any doubts or questions.
3. **Project Scope and Timeline:** Clearly define the scope of work for the project, including specific tasks, deadlines, and deliverables. Make sure both you and your client have a mutual understanding of the project objectives.
4. **Communication Channels:** Establish preferred communication channels with your client, such as email, messaging platforms, or project management tools. Clearly communicate response times and availability to set expectations for ongoing communication.
5. **Access and Permissions:** Obtain any necessary access or permissions

required to perform your tasks effectively. This may include access to client systems, databases, or social media accounts.
6. **Training and Knowledge Transfer:** If required, provide training to the client on how to use specific tools or systems that you will be utilizing. Ensure they have the knowledge they need to collaborate effectively with you.

Setting Client Expectations

During the onboarding process, it's crucial to set clear expectations with your clients. Here's what to focus on:

- **Availability and Response Times:** Clearly communicate your availability, response times, and preferred modes of communication.
- **Potential Challenges:** Discuss any potential challenges or limitations that may arise during the project and how they will be addressed.
- **Feedback and Revisions:** Establish guidelines for feedback and revisions. Clearly outline the number of revisions included in the agreed-upon package and any additional charges for revisions beyond that scope. This will prevent

misunderstandings and ensure a smoother working relationship.

Managing Projects Effectively

Once the onboarding process is complete, it's time to focus on managing projects efficiently. Effective project management ensures client satisfaction, timely delivery of work, and overall success for your virtual assistant business.

Establishing a Project Management System

Consider implementing a project management system to streamline your workflow and enhance collaboration with your clients. Popular project management tools include Trello, Asana, and Basecamp. These tools allow you to create tasks, set deadlines, communicate with clients, and track progress.

Communication and Progress Updates

Maintaining regular and clear communication with your clients is vital throughout the project. Provide frequent progress updates, discuss any challenges or roadblocks, and seek feedback to ensure you remain aligned with the client's expectations.

Managing Time and Prioritizing Tasks

As a virtual assistant, efficient time management is crucial. Create a schedule or use time-tracking tools to block time for different tasks, prioritizing urgent projects. Regularly review your task list to ensure you are on track and meeting deadlines.

Delivering High-Quality Work

Consistently delivering high-quality work is essential to maintain client satisfaction. Pay attention to detail, proofread your work, and ensure it aligns with the client's instructions and requirements. Strive for excellence in every task you complete.

Conclusion

Onboarding clients effectively and managing projects efficiently are critical aspects of running a successful virtual assistant business. By establishing a streamlined onboarding process, setting clear client expectations, and implementing proper project management techniques, you can ensure client satisfaction and achieve long-term success.

Chapter 7: Delivering High-Quality Services

To build a successful virtual assistant business, focusing on delivering high-quality services is essential. Exceptional work leads to satisfied clients, positive referrals, and a solid reputation in the industry. Let's dive into some key strategies to help you consistently deliver top-notch services as a virtual assistant.

1. Understand Client Expectations

Before starting any project, it's crucial to clearly understand your client's expectations. Take the time to communicate thoroughly and gather all necessary information about the project scope, desired outcomes, and any specific instructions or preferences they may have. This ensures you're on the same page and can deliver work that meets or exceeds their expectations.

2. Maintain Open and Regular Communication

Communication is the backbone of any successful business relationship, and as a virtual assistant, it's even more critical. Keep the lines of communication open with your clients throughout the project. Regularly update them on your progress, seek clarification when needed, and provide timely responses to any queries or concerns. This level of communication builds trust, shows your commitment to the project, and ensures you're effectively meeting their needs.

3. Pay Attention to Detail

In the virtual assistant world, attention to detail is paramount. Take the time to review your work meticulously, checking for any errors or inconsistencies. Ensure that your deliverables are professionally presented, properly formatted, and tailored to the client's requirements. By paying close attention to detail, you demonstrate your professionalism and dedication to delivering high-quality work.

4. Meet Deadlines

Timeliness is crucial when delivering services. As a virtual assistant, you must establish realistic timelines and consistently meet the agreed-upon deadlines. If unexpected circumstances arise that may cause a delay, communicate with your client in advance and offer alternative solutions or revised timelines. This proactive approach shows your commitment to delivering quality work within the agreed-upon timeframes.

5. Continuous Improvement

To consistently deliver high-quality services, invest in your professional development. Stay updated with industry trends, new tools, and techniques. Take online courses, attend webinars, or join professional associations to enhance your skills and stay ahead of the curve. Continuously improving your knowledge and skills enables you to provide the best possible services to your clients.

6. Solicit and Act on Feedback

Feedback is an invaluable tool for improving your services. Encourage your clients to provide feedback on your work, communication, and overall experience. Actively listen to their feedback, identify areas for improvement, and take necessary steps to address any shortcomings. By demonstrating your willingness to evolve and grow based on feedback, you show your clients that their opinions are valued, and it builds trust in your ability to deliver exceptional services.

Conclusion

Delivering high-quality services is essential for establishing a successful virtual assistant business. By understanding client expectations, maintaining open communication, paying attention to detail, meeting deadlines, continuously improving your skills, and soliciting and acting on feedback, you can consistently deliver exceptional work. Your commitment to delivering high-quality services will not only satisfy your current clients but also attract new clients and help you build a solid reputation in the industry.

Chapter 8: Scaling Your Virtual Assistant Business

Scaling your virtual assistant business is an exciting journey that involves expanding your operations to handle more clients and boost your revenue. It allows you to take on additional clients, offer a broader range of services, and possibly build a team of virtual assistants to support your growing business. However, scaling requires meticulous planning and strategy to ensure a seamless transition while maintaining the quality of your services. Let's dive into some key steps to help you scale your virtual assistant business successfully.

Evaluate Your Current Capacity

Before you embark on scaling, it's crucial to assess your current capacity to manage an increased workload. Take a realistic look at your resources, including your time, skills, and technology. Can you accommodate more clients without compromising the quality of your service? If you find gaps, consider upgrading your technology or enhancing your skills to handle the growing demand. This self-assessment will provide a clear picture of where you stand and what improvements are necessary.

Streamline Your Processes

Efficiency is the backbone of a scalable business. To streamline your virtual assistant business, identify and eliminate inefficiencies or bottlenecks in your workflow. Look for repetitive tasks that can be automated using productivity tools or consider outsourcing certain tasks to free up your time for higher-value projects. By optimizing your processes, you can manage more clients without sacrificing the quality of your service. Think of it as setting the foundation for a more robust and efficient business operation.

Expand Your Service Offerings

To attract new clients and retain existing ones, think about expanding your service offerings. Identify areas of expertise or complementary services that align with your current offerings and meet market demand. Conduct market research to understand the needs and preferences of your target audience. By diversifying your services, you can appeal to a broader range of clients and create additional revenue streams. This expansion can also position you as a one-stop solution for your clients' various needs.

Develop a Marketing Strategy

Scaling your business requires a solid marketing strategy to reach a wider audience. Develop a comprehensive marketing plan that includes digital marketing tactics such as search engine optimization (SEO), content marketing, social media marketing, and email marketing. Create compelling content that showcases your expertise and highlights the benefits of working with your virtual assistant business. Utilize platforms like LinkedIn, industry-specific forums, and online communities to expand your reach and attract more clients. Effective marketing is essential to build your brand and drive business growth.

Hire Additional Virtual Assistants

As your client base grows, consider hiring additional virtual assistants to support your business. Look for individuals with complementary skills and expertise who can handle specific tasks or services. Develop a rigorous hiring process to ensure you select qualified candidates who align with your business values and work ethic. Provide thorough training and clear guidelines to ensure consistency in service quality across your team. Building a reliable team is key to managing a larger client base effectively.

Implement Systems for Scalability

To scale your virtual assistant business effectively, invest in systems and tools that support scalability. Adopt project management software to handle multiple clients simultaneously and enhance collaboration within your team. Implement a customer relationship management (CRM) system to track and manage client interactions efficiently. Regularly evaluate your technology stack and consider upgrading or integrating new tools as needed to streamline processes and improve productivity. Scalable systems will help you manage growth smoothly and maintain high service standards.

Foster Client Relationships

Maintaining strong client relationships is essential for scaling your virtual assistant business. Continuously communicate with your clients, seek feedback, and proactively address any concerns or issues. Offer personalized and tailored solutions to meet their evolving needs. Nurture long-term relationships by going above and beyond to exceed client expectations. Happy and satisfied clients will not only stay with your business but also refer new clients, contributing to your growth. Strong client relationships are the cornerstone of a thriving business.

Conclusion

Scaling your virtual assistant business requires careful planning, efficient processes, and a customer-centric approach. By evaluating your capacity, streamlining processes, expanding service offerings, developing a marketing strategy, hiring additional virtual assistants, implementing scalable systems, and fostering client relationships, you can successfully scale your virtual assistant business to achieve long-term growth and profitability. Continuously monitor and adapt your strategies to stay ahead in a competitive market. Embrace the journey of scaling with confidence, knowing that each step brings you closer to building a successful and sustainable business.

Chapter 9: Navigating Challenges and Overcoming Obstacles

Welcome to Chapter 9. As a virtual assistant, you'll inevitably face various challenges and obstacles along your journey. But don't worry—with the right mindset and strategies, you can navigate these challenges and come out stronger on the other side. In this chapter, we'll explore some common challenges faced by virtual assistants and discuss effective strategies to overcome them.

Dealing with Time Management Issues

One of the biggest challenges for virtual assistants is managing time effectively. Without proper time management, you might struggle to meet deadlines, feel overwhelmed with tasks, and experience work-life balance issues. Here are some strategies to help you tackle this challenge:

Establish a Routine

Creating a daily or weekly schedule that outlines specific time blocks for client work, administrative tasks, and personal activities can make a big difference. Stick to this routine as much as possible to increase productivity and maintain a sense of structure.

Prioritize Tasks

Determine which tasks are most important and urgent. Focus on completing these tasks first before moving on to others. You can use prioritization techniques like the Eisenhower Matrix to help identify tasks that can be delegated or eliminated.

Utilize Time-Management Tools

Leverage technology tools and apps that can help you track your time, set reminders, and organize your tasks. Some popular time-management tools include Trello, Asana, and RescueTime. These tools can be lifesavers when it comes to keeping everything on track.

Managing Client Expectations

Clear communication and managing client expectations are crucial to maintaining a successful virtual assistant business. Here's how you can navigate this challenge:

Set Realistic Expectations

From the start, be transparent with your clients about what you can deliver and the timeframe in which you can do so. Avoid overpromising and underdelivering, as this can damage your reputation. Be honest and set achievable goals.

Clarify Scope of Work

Clearly define the scope of work in your client agreements and establish boundaries. Regularly communicate with your clients to ensure they understand what tasks are included in your services and what falls outside of your responsibilities. This will prevent any confusion down the line.

Regularly Communicate

Maintain open lines of communication with your clients throughout the project. Provide progress updates, ask for feedback, and address any concerns in a timely manner. Effective communication helps build trust and prevents misunderstandings.

Handling Difficult Clients

Every now and then, you might encounter challenging clients. Here are some tips for handling difficult situations:

Stay Calm and Professional

When faced with a difficult client, it's important to remain calm and professional. Avoid reacting defensively or taking things personally. Focus on finding solutions and maintaining a positive working relationship.

Active Listening

Listen to your client's concerns or frustrations without interrupting. Let them express themselves fully before responding. This shows that you value their feedback and are dedicated to addressing their concerns.

Offer Solutions
Instead of dwelling on the problem, focus on finding solutions. Brainstorm ideas and present them to the client. Collaborate to identify a resolution that meets their needs while aligning with your capabilities.

Balancing Work and Personal Life
Achieving a healthy work-life balance is essential for your well-being and long-term success as a virtual assistant. Here are some strategies to help you find that balance:

Set Boundaries
Establish clear boundaries between your work and personal life. Determine specific work hours and stick to them. Communicate these boundaries to your clients and loved ones, and encourage their respect and understanding.

Take Regular Breaks
Allow yourself to take regular breaks throughout the day. Step away from your computer, stretch, and engage in activities that help you relax and recharge. This will prevent burnout and increase your overall productivity.

Delegate and Outsource

If you find yourself overwhelmed with work, consider delegating or outsourcing tasks that are not your core competencies. This will give you more time to focus on high-value tasks and enjoy a better work-life balance.

By navigating these challenges and implementing effective strategies, you can overcome obstacles and thrive in your virtual assistant business. Remember, challenges are opportunities for growth and learning. Embrace them, adapt, and continue to improve. You've got this!

Chapter 10: Sustaining Success and Long-Term Growth

Achieving success is just the beginning; sustaining it and fostering long-term growth are the true goals for any virtual assistant business. Once you've built a solid foundation and attracted clients, it's essential to focus on strategies that will help you maintain and expand your business. In this chapter, we'll explore various tactics and approaches that can help you sustain success and achieve long-term growth in your virtual assistant business.

Evaluate Your Current Capacity

As your business grows, it's important to periodically evaluate your capacity to handle client work. Assess whether your current workload is manageable and determine if you need additional resources, such as hiring more virtual assistants. This evaluation will help you identify areas where you may need to streamline processes or make adjustments to ensure you can meet client demands effectively.

Streamline Your Processes

Efficiency is crucial for sustaining success and achieving long-term growth. Take the time to review your existing processes and identify areas where you can streamline workflows. Look for repetitive tasks that can be automated, invest in tools and software that can improve productivity, and eliminate any unnecessary steps in your processes. By streamlining your operations, you can optimize your time and resources, allowing you to take on more clients and deliver exceptional results.

Expand Your Service Offerings

To sustain success and drive long-term growth, consider expanding your service offerings. Conduct market research to identify emerging trends and demands within the virtual assistant industry. This will help you determine which additional services you can offer that align with your skills and expertise. By diversifying your service offerings, you can attract a wider range of clients and create new revenue streams for your business.

Develop a Marketing Strategy

A strong marketing strategy is essential for sustaining your success and achieving long-term growth. Identify your target audience and develop a comprehensive marketing plan that includes both online and offline tactics. Leverage digital channels such as social media, email marketing, and content creation to build brand awareness and attract potential clients. Additionally, consider attending industry-specific conferences and events to network with potential clients and showcase your expertise.

Hire Additional Virtual Assistants

As your client base expands, you may need to hire additional virtual assistants to handle the workload. Carefully assess your hiring needs and identify candidates who possess the skills and experience required to provide high-quality services to your clients. Implement a thorough recruitment process, including conducting interviews and assessing candidates' portfolios and references. By hiring competent and reliable virtual assistants, you can effectively scale your business and accommodate a larger client base.

Implement Systems for Scalability

To sustain success and achieve long-term growth, it's important to implement systems and processes that are scalable. This includes investing in project management tools, communication platforms, and other software that can enhance collaboration with clients and virtual assistants. Establish clear guidelines and standard operating procedures to ensure consistency and efficiency in your service delivery. By implementing scalable systems, you can effectively manage increased workloads and maintain the quality of your services as your business grows.

Foster Client Relationships

Maintaining strong and positive client relationships is essential for sustaining long-term success. Regularly communicate with your clients, provide progress updates, and ensure that their needs and expectations are being met. Seek feedback from your clients and implement any necessary improvements or adjustments. By fostering strong relationships, you can cultivate client loyalty and generate repeat business.

Conclusion: Scaling Requires Planning, Efficiency, Customer Focus, Monitoring, and Adaptation

Sustaining success and achieving long-term growth in a virtual assistant business requires careful planning, efficient processes, a customer-focused approach, continuous monitoring, and adaptability. By constantly assessing your capacity, streamlining processes, expanding services, developing a marketing strategy, hiring additional virtual assistants, implementing scalable systems, and fostering client relationships, you will position your business for sustained success and future growth.

Conclusion: Embracing the Future as a Virtual Assistant

As we conclude "The Ultimate Guide on How To Start a Virtual Assistant Business," you've traversed the comprehensive pathway from understanding the basics of virtual assistance in Chapter 1 to sustaining long-term growth and success in Chapter 10. This journey has equipped you with the essential tools, knowledge, and strategies to launch and expand your own virtual assistant business effectively.

Recap of Our Journey

- Chapter 1 introduced you to the world of virtual assistance, setting the stage for what it means to be a virtual assistant and the vast opportunities within this industry.
- Chapter 2 helped you assess your own skills and determine the services you can offer, ensuring you have a solid foundation to build your business upon.
- Chapter 3 walked you through the crucial steps of setting up your virtual assistant business, covering everything

from legal considerations to establishing your online presence.
- Chapter 4 focused on finding your first clients, offering strategies to attract and secure your initial contracts and start building your professional reputation.
- Chapter 5 discussed establishing your pricing and packages, guiding you on how to value your services competitively yet fairly to attract a wide range of clients.
- Chapter 6 dove into onboarding clients and managing projects efficiently, ensuring smooth operations and client satisfaction.
- Chapter 7 emphasized the importance of delivering high-quality services, which is pivotal to maintaining positive client relationships and fostering referrals.
- Chapter 8 explored strategies for scaling your business, providing insights into how to expand your services and client base without compromising quality.
- Chapter 9 addressed the inevitable challenges and obstacles you will face and offered advice on how to navigate these issues gracefully and effectively.
- Chapter 10 closed our exploration by focusing on sustaining success and ensuring long-term growth, critical for a thriving and resilient business.

Forging Ahead

Now that you are equipped with a robust set of tools and insights, your journey as a virtual assistant is just beginning. Here are a few key points to keep in mind as you move forward:

- Stay adaptable: The virtual assistance field is dynamic and ever-changing. Staying adaptable and open to learning new skills and technologies will keep you competitive and in demand.
- Prioritize communication: Effective communication is crucial in a virtual setting. Ensure clear, concise, and regular interactions with your clients to build trust and maintain a professional relationship.
- Focus on quality: As your business grows, maintain the high standard of services that you've set. Quality is what will distinguish you from the competition and drive customer satisfaction.
- Seek feedback: Regularly ask for feedback from your clients. This will not only help you improve your services but also reinforce your clients' satisfaction with your business.
- Plan for growth: Use the strategies discussed in Chapter 8 to carefully plan your business expansion. Remember, sustainable growth is about smart

scaling that aligns with your long-term business goals.

Thank you for choosing this guide as your roadmap to starting a virtual assistant business. Your dedication to mastering the nuances of virtual assistance will no doubt be a cornerstone of your success. Here's to your future achievements, where your skills, professionalism, and entrepreneurial spirit lead you to remarkable places in the expanding digital landscape. Let's embrace the future with enthusiasm and confidence as you build and grow your virtual assistant business.

www.ingramcontent.com/pod-product-compliance
Lightning Source LLC
Chambersburg PA
CBHW070133230526
45472CB00004B/1525